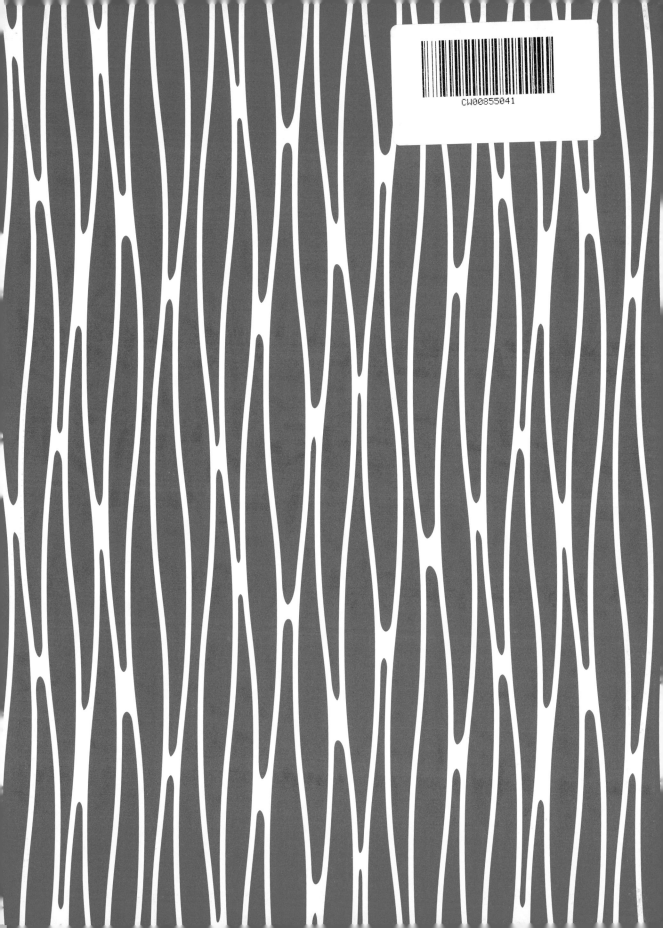

CW00855041

BURP, SPIT & FART

Inspiring | Educating | Creating | Entertaining

Brimming with creative inspiration, how-to projects, and useful information to enrich your everyday life, Quarto Knows is a favorite destination for those pursuing their interests and passions. Visit our site and dig deeper with our books into your area of interest: Quarto Creates, Quarto Cooks, Quarto Homes, Quarto Lives, Quarto Drives, Quarto Explores, Quarto Gifts, or Quarto Kids.

Young Voyageur Press titles are also available at discount for retail, wholesale, promotional, and bulk purchase. For details, contact the Special Sales Manager by email at specialsales@quarto.com or by mail at The Quarto Group, Attn: Special Sales Manager, 100 Cummings Center Suite 265D, Beverly, MA 01915 USA.

10 9 8 7 6 5 4 3 2 1

ISBN: 978-0-7603-6476-5

Digital edition published in 2018
eISBN: 978-0-7603-6477-2

Library of Congress Cataloging-in-Publication Data

Names: Garstecki, Julia, author. | Monroe, Chris, illustrator.
Title: Burp, spit & fart : the science behind the gross things babies do /
words by Julia Garstecki ; illustrations by Chris Monroe.
Description: Minneapolis, Minnesota : Young Voyageur Press, 2019. | Audience: Ages 8-12.
Identifiers: LCCN 2018051033 | ISBN 9780760364765 (paper over board)
Subjects: LCSH: Infants--Behavior--Juvenile literature. |
Infants--Physiology--Juvenile literature. | Brothers and sisters--Juvenile literature.
Classification: LCC HQ774 .G3545 2019 | DDC 155.42/2--dc23
LC record available at https://lccn.loc.gov/2018051033

Acquiring Editor: Dennis Pernu
Project Managers: Alyssa Lochner and Alyssa Bluhm
Art Director: Cindy Samargia Laun

The artwork in the book is done in gouache and ink on watercolor paper.

Printed in China

MIX
Paper from responsible sources
FSC® C008047

BURP, SPIT & FART

The SCIENCE Behind the GROSS Things Babies Do

Words by Julia Garstecki   Illustrations by Chris Monroe

young voyageur

SO . . . THERE'S A NEW BABY IN YOUR LIFE!

Maybe you just became a big brother or sister. Maybe you have a new baby cousin. Or maybe a neighbor or your mom's best friend just had a baby. Wherever there's a baby, it usually means a big celebration. That's because a new baby is a reason to celebrate! Babies come with teeny-tiny eyelashes and toes smaller than beans. They make cute faces and yawn and babble. They smell so good . . . most of the time.

BRAP

But a new baby can be kind of gross too. They don't do much except sleep and cry. Then they burp and poop in public and don't even get in any trouble.

As babies grow, some of their **behaviors** will change. Let's learn all about these baby behaviors. Then you'll be ready to help the baby in your life grow up to be as awesome as you.

Gross.

About 350,000 babies are born each day around the world. That's 4.3 babies born every second!

5

WHAT THE HECK HAPPENED IN THERE?

When you are waiting for a baby sister or brother to be born, it can feel like forever! That's because it takes a long time to grow a baby.

It's hard to imagine, but each of us was once inside our mom's belly. Everyone started with a tiny cell called an **egg** inside our mothers. That single egg then divided into groups of cells. Some cells formed your heart. Others became your bones. Still others became your brain, which lets you think, feel, and act.

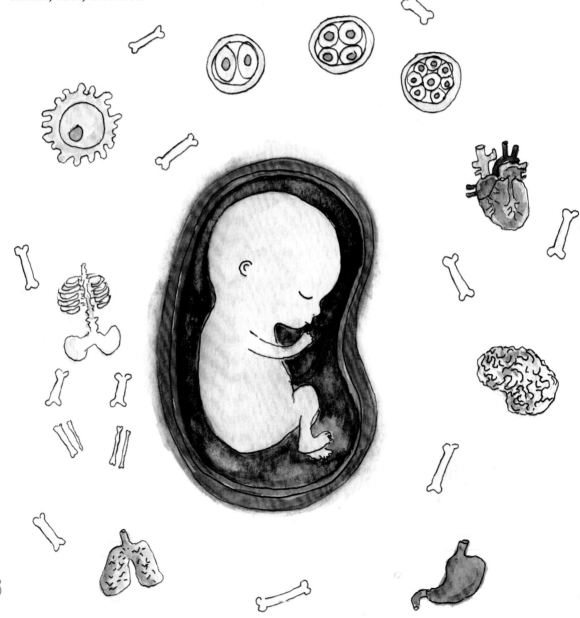

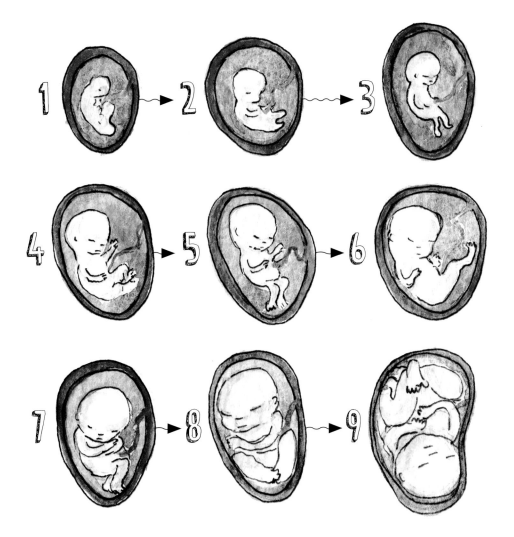

After one month inside the mother's **womb**, a baby is still smaller than a grain of rice. But each month the baby grows. After nine months, she is ready to live outside Mother. That's when most mothers go to a hospital. There, nurses and doctors help **deliver** the baby.

Now that the baby is here, what happens next?

Parents (and siblings!) can see pictures of the baby before it is born. These pictures are called "sonograms." Doctors use them to see if the baby is healthy.

THE FIRST THREE YEARS

The Brain

During the first three years of life, a baby's brain develops quickly. The baby **senses** new things each day. These experiences help his brain grow.

A baby is born with about 100 billion brain cells! Brain cells work alone at first. As a baby repeats activities, the brain cells begin working together and forming networks.

As baby's body grows, she learns how to use it. Now that you're older, you can climb stairs and tell a joke. That wasn't always the case. These were things you learned and practiced.

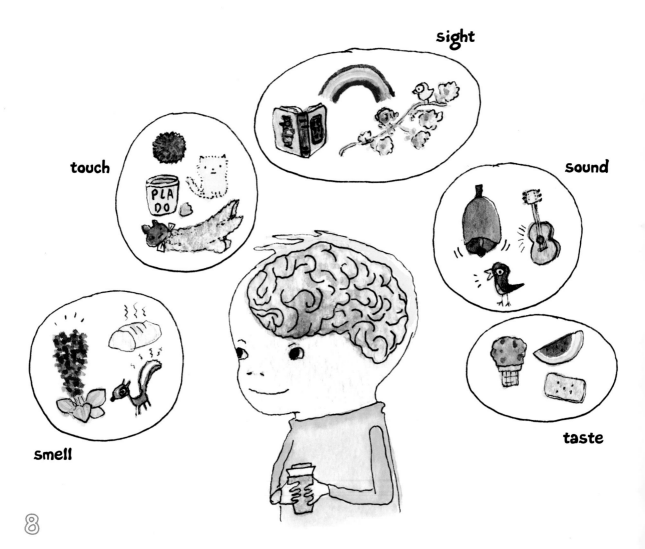

sight

touch

sound

smell

taste

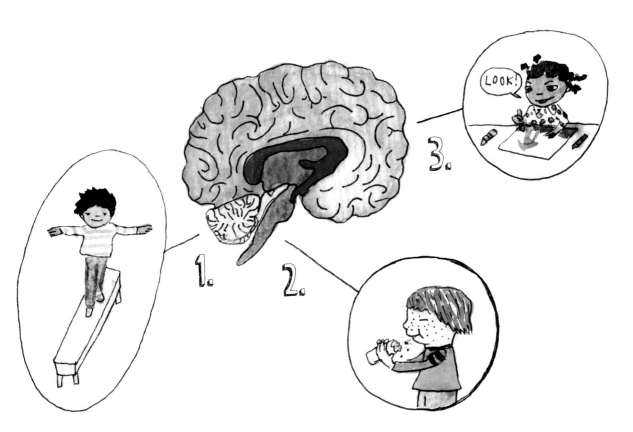

Parts of the Brain

Different parts of the brain control different abilities:

1. **Cerebellum** – affects balance and posture
2. **Brain stem** – takes care of things you don't even realize you're doing, like breathing and digestion
3. **Cerebrum** – the largest part of the brain allows us to feel, touch, see, hear, and speak, and control little movements like holding a crayon

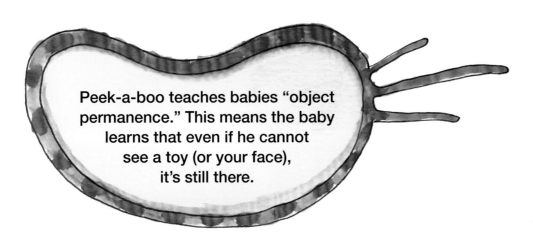

Peek-a-boo teaches babies "object permanence." This means the baby learns that even if he cannot see a toy (or your face), it's still there.

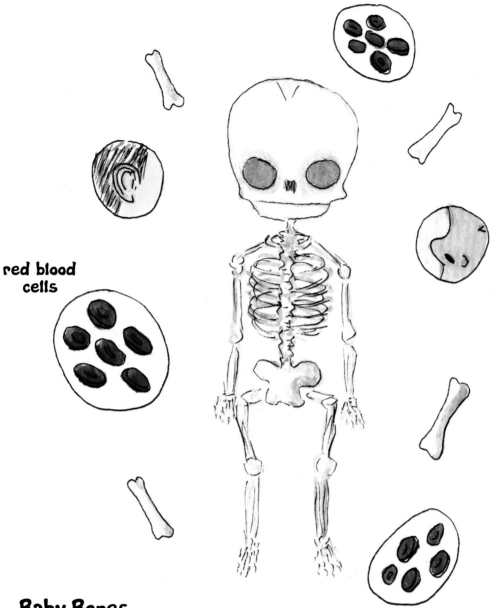

red blood
cells

Baby Bones

We might think of bones as dry and clattery, but they actually grow and change. They also give you support and make red blood cells that carry oxygen throughout your body.

Babies are born with about 300 bones. Many bones start as softer **cartilage**—the same stuff your nose and ears are made of. This allows new bones to be flexible when the baby is still in mom's tummy. After birth, some bones fuse. An adult human has only 206 bones.

fontanelle

There's something even more amazing about baby bones. Newborn babies have two soft spots in their heads. One is at the back and the other is on top.

These soft spots are called **fontanelles**. They are spaces between the bones of the skull. Fontanelles allow a baby's head to change shape when the baby is being delivered! As the baby grows, doctors check these soft spots to make sure the skull is growing correctly.

Fontanelles usually close in 12 to 18 months. They also allow the baby's brain to grow.

11

SLEEP AND THE NEW BABY

Being a baby is tiring work. Newborns sleep up to 18 hours a day! They usually sleep for just a few hours at a time. It might seem like babies are lazy, but the brain and body need time to rest so babies can learn.

Researchers have discovered that as babies sleep, they build connections between their brains' sides.

The brain's left side controls the right side of the body. It is also helps us do science and math tasks. The brain's right side controls the left side of the body. It helps with creativity.

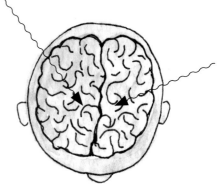

Babies might wake up four or five times a night. In fact, most babies don't sleep through the night until they are at least three months old. Some babies take as much as a year before they sleep through the night! This is why new parents often walk around like zombies!

Newborns require a lot of sleep, but so do seniors. This is why grandma might snooze so much . . . just like when she was a baby!

THE STAGES OF SLEEP

Sometimes a sleeping baby is very, very still. Other times he is more active, kicking or making funny faces.

REM sleep (rapid eye movement sleep) is a deep sleep stage. It is when dreams happen. During this stage, you might see his eyes moving beneath those little lids. He'll probably pee or poo while he sleeps too.

Never put small toys or soft objects in a crib with a baby! They can block a baby's breathing if she rolls onto them. Babies should sleep on their back on a firm (but not hard) surface.

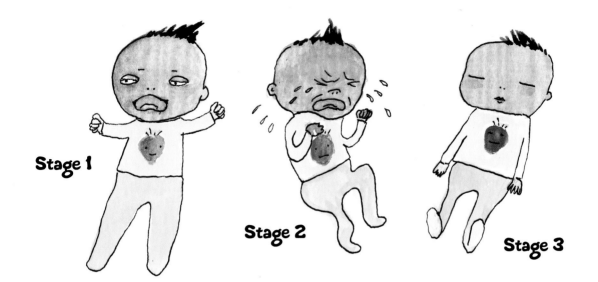

Stage 1

Stage 2

Stage 3

Non-REM sleep has three stages.

First comes drowsiness, when babies start to doze. They may get super cuddly and yawn cute baby yawns. Then they slip into stage two, a light sleep, usually with no dreams. In this stage the baby will still startle if she hears loud sounds. She might cry and have a hard time going back to sleep.

When the baby enters stage three of non-REM sleep, she has fallen into a deep sleep. She will be very quiet and not move. You might even be able to play and still not wake her up!

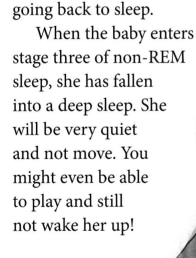

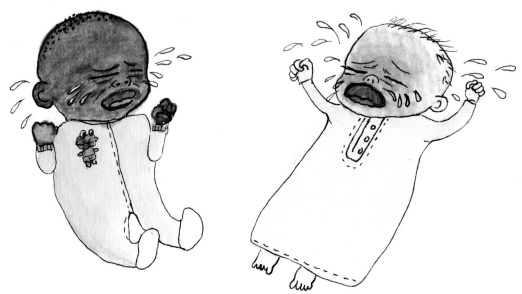

CRY BABIES

Instead of saying "I would like to eat" or "My diaper is full," a baby cries.

The more you get to know that little fella, the more you might notice different cries. Some new parents spend huge amounts of time learning what each cry means.

Parents try hard to comfort crying babies—especially if it's the middle of the night. Or on an airplane. Sometimes the crying lasts only a moment. Other times, a baby will cry for hours! Yes . . . hours!

REASONS BABIES CRY

I'm hungry
My diaper is dirty
I'm hot
I'm cold
I want snuggles
I want to be left alone
I'm gassy

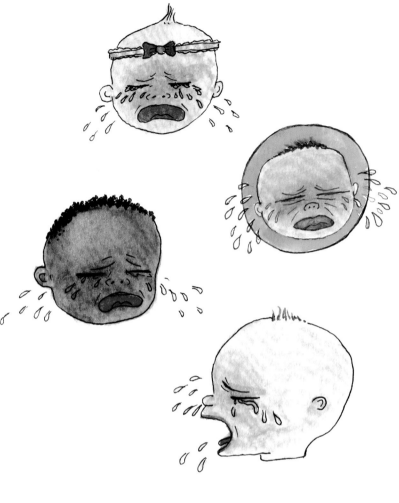

Sometimes babies cry because they are tired. While it might be fun to make a baby laugh, he also needs calm time. Rocking, turning off lights, and humming can help him relax.

Crying babies can be frustrating. Just have patience and remember they are trying to tell us something.

IT TAKES GUTS

The **digestive system** is amazing. There, the human body turns your favorite food into nutrients it needs to grow. Then your body gets rid of the stuff it doesn't use.

Digestive systems begin forming when you're still inside your mother. The system starts as a bunch of tubes. As the baby grows inside Mom, these tubes turn into **organs**, like the stomach and intestines.

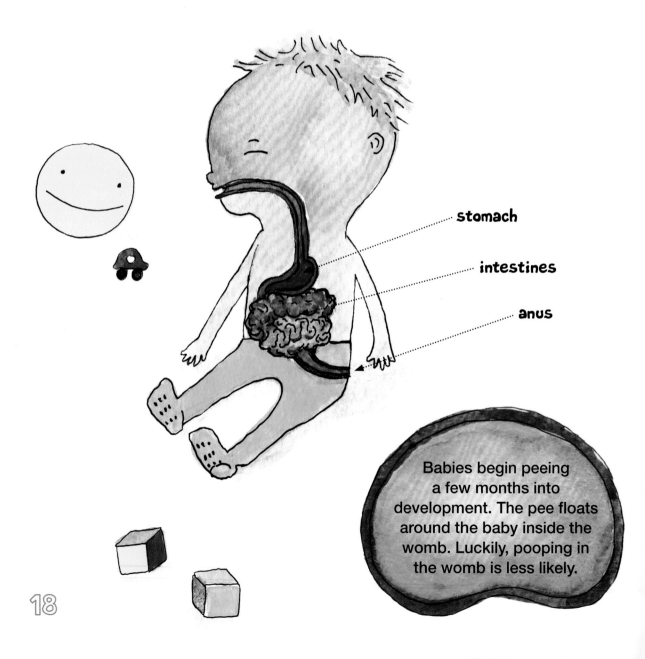

stomach

intestines

anus

Babies begin peeing a few months into development. The pee floats around the baby inside the womb. Luckily, pooping in the womb is less likely.

At three days old, a baby's stomach is about the size of a Ping-Pong ball. At ten days, it has grown to the size of a chicken egg. Even when she's a month old, a baby's tummy can only hold 4 ounces (118 milliliters) of liquid. An adult stomach can hold more than 110 ounces (3.3 liters) of liquid.

So, a baby can't put much in there. Instead, they eat a little at a time many times a day. And because their digestive systems are so small, most babies digest their food quickly and poop soon after eating.

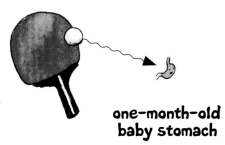

one-month-old baby stomach

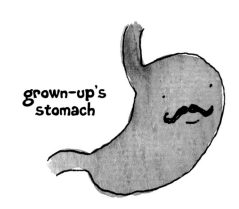

grown-up's stomach

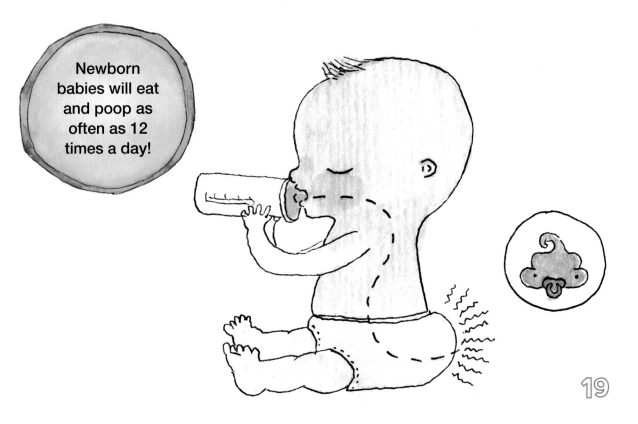

Newborn babies will eat and poop as often as 12 times a day!

WHAT DOES THIS THING EAT?

Even though babies eat a lot, they can't break out the chips and salsa just yet. They can't even slurp up mushy overcooked noodles.

So what do babies eat? Well, babies need a lot of nutrients that they can digest easily. They get these nutrients from milk.

But the milk babies drink isn't the milk you and I drink. It comes either from the mother or is **formula** from the store. Special fats in mother's milk and formula help the baby's brain, eyes, and nervous system develop. Other nutrients help fight diseases.

Most doctors say babies shouldn't eat solid food until they're six months old. That's because solid foods aren't as nutritious as breast milk or formula. Plus, babies can't chew or swallow solid foods.

Babies weigh about 5 to 9 pounds (2.3 to 4.1 kilograms) when they're born. In about six months, they double their size. What if we doubled our size twice in one year?

GROWNUP FOOD

When they are four to six months old, babies can finally hold their heads up on their own. They have also figured out how to use their tongues. And they're probably hungry more often. This means they are ready for solid food.

Many parents start by giving their babies cereal made with rice, oats, or barley. It's gray and looks like mush. To you, it will taste boring. But babies can't have foods with lots of salt or sugar. Luckily, they've never had pizza and don't know what they're missing!

Babies may have more taste buds than adults. Even so, they can't taste salt until they are about four months old.

A baby's first solid food will likely depend on where she lives.

In Japan, many infants eat fish by their first birthday. But in the United States, most doctors tell parents to wait until after a child's first birthday before letting them eat fish.

In Kenya, mashed sweet potatoes are introduced early. Swedish babies are fed something called *välling*, a thick, syrupy drink like the thin rice cereal babies in the United States eat.

In Great Britain and France, mashed veggies are a solid food for babies. In Jamaica, it's mashed-up fruits.

BRAP

LETTING AIR OUT

You might notice that new parents are fussy about burping their baby.

A burp releases gas bubbles out of your mouth. Because babies swallow air when they eat, suck a pacifier (or fingers), and laugh, air gets trapped in their digestive sustems. Burping a baby helps the air escape. If a baby isn't burped every few minutes while eating, he can get a tummy ache.

Some babies also get the hiccups when they eat. Many babies even hiccup when they're still inside their mothers!

Hiccups are strong, sudden movements of the **diaphragm**, a muscle that helps you breathe. They don't hurt, but they can be annoying. Babies can get hiccups if they are overfed or need to be burped. Once a baby grows a bit, his hiccups will likely decrease.

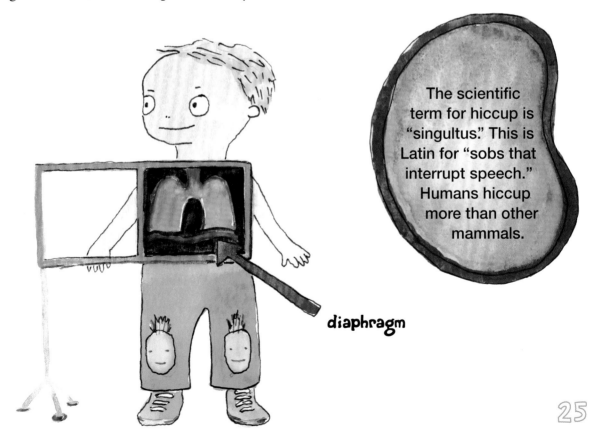

diaphragm

The scientific term for hiccup is "singultus." This is Latin for "sobs that interrupt speech." Humans hiccup more than other mammals.

THE TRUTH ABOUT SPIT-UP

Spit-up is super-gross. It is kind of like vomit—a liquid mix of milk and saliva.

How does it work? A valve between the esophagus and the stomach keeps food in the stomach, where it belongs. But a baby's valve isn't yet developed. As the infant grows, this valve gets stronger. Until then, if a baby eats too quickly or needs to be burped, he could very well spit up.

Babies will also spit up if they eat too much. After all, their tummies are tiny!

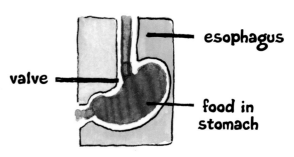

esophagus

valve

food in stomach

If you're in charge of helping feed a new baby, your chances of being covered in baby spit-up decrease if you burp the baby every few minutes and hold the baby in an upright position. Definitely do *not* bounce the baby while she eats!

Spit-up isn't exactly vomit. It's more like a leak. Vomit, on the other hand, is more of a forceful explosion of digested food. Luckily, vomiting is rare for babies.

CUTIE PUH-TOOT-IE!

We've seen that gas can escape babies in burps and hiccups. Well, if the gas doesn't escape from above, it will escape from below!

Babies are so cute. They sleep, they sigh, they smile. Then suddenly, BWAHHHT!!! That cute little fella lets one rip! Why?

The muscles that push a baby's food down into its digestive system are still weak. Also, they don't yet have all the good **bacteria** that helps them digest their food. These are two reasons why Cutie-Patootie will be a gas factory.

TOOT

BWAHHT

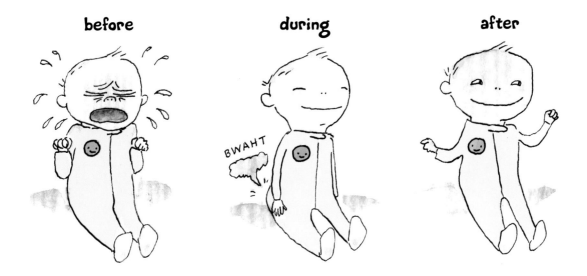

before during after

GAS AND CRYING

Remember the last time you had a belly ache? If you let loose a good fart, you probably felt some relief! Babies don't know that we think farts are disgusting and embarrassing. And they sure don't know how to hold it in until they are in a private place. They just fart away whenever they need to.
Sometimes, when a baby has a belly ache,
a good fart will solve the problem.

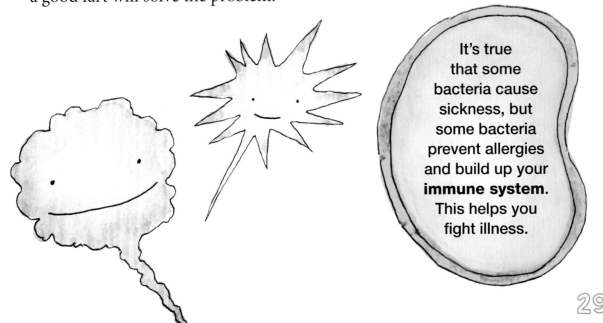

It's true that some bacteria cause sickness, but some bacteria prevent allergies and build up your **immune system.** This helps you fight illness.

You should go POOP!

You need to eat MORE VEGGIES!

ALL ABOUT POOP

Grownups seem to be poop experts. Say you have a stomachache, and they'll tell you to go poop. Tell them your poop's hard, and they'll say that you need to eat more veggies.

A lot of grownups even know that a baby's first poop is called **meconium**. It's greenish-black and sticky. Meconium is made up of **mucus**, old skin and blood cells, and even little hairs the baby shed while growing.

After a baby is born, her poop will lighten to an army green color. This means her intestines are working.

Some babies make a big deal about filling their diaper with that stuff. They squish their face up tight, causing their whole head to get red. They grunt as they push.

Other babies stare off into the distance, as if they are posing for a picture. Some babies even smile as the odor inches across the room. It's another amusing behavior babies grow out of.

Did you know some moms can pick out the smell of their baby's poop? In scientific studies, many moms identified their babies' poop smell from a group of dirty diapers.

THE POOP DETECTIVES

Poop comes in colors from yellow to green to brown to black. When a baby starts to eat solid food, his poop begins look more like the poop you make—brown and thick. Brown poop gets its color from **bile** that is pumped into the stomach. The bile is green or yellow at first. It gets darker as it moves through the digestive system. A greenish turd means the poo moved quickly through the system.

Poop has many smells too. Sometimes you won't even realize there's a doodie in the diaper. Other times your eyes will water and you might gag. The smell usually depends on how long the poop was in the intestines. The longer it sits in there, the worse it will smell.

Sooner or later, all new parents learn about diaper blow out! Sometimes babies can have such a huge bowel movement that poop runs up their backs and even into their hair!

33

  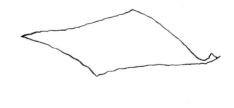

THE INCREDIBLE DIAPER

In ancient times, babies were wrapped in leaves or animal skins. In warmer climates, they were often left naked. Eventually, cloth diapers were developed. However, these need to be washed after each poop or pee. In fact, before indoor washing machines, many people didn't even wash cloth diapers. They just dried and reused them!

Today, disposable diapers are simply thrown away when they're dirty. Disposable diapers have three layers to absorb pee. Inside, little beads called "polymers" (PAUL-a-murs) absorb pee. The beads then swell up and look like gel-filled marbles. You can see them if you rip open a wet diaper.

In the United States, 20 billion disposable diapers are thrown into the garbage every year. These diapers can end up in landfills, where it takes up to 500 years for them to **degrade**!

LANDFILL

35

TINKLE TIME

Peeing on the potty takes a lot of practice. When the bladder is full, it sends messages the brain, saying that it needs to be emptied. The body needs to know how to hold the pee inside until we find a toilet and it's okay to let the pee go!

Tinkle

Tinkle

Tinkle

Tinkle

It's the same with pooping. Nerves in your **rectum** tell the brain that you have to poop or maybe fart to relieve some pressure. It takes time for the muscles that hold in pee and poop to work well with the brain. That's one reason why babies need diapers. Even older kids can think they're going to fart but end up pooping instead. These accidents happen all the time!

If you or your baby brother have trouble pooping, drink more water and eat more veggies. This will make for stronger, healthier poop!

CLEANING A WIGGLY BABY

With all this spit-up, poop, and pee, babies can get pretty messy.

Luckily, your baby brother doesn't need a bath every day. If he did have a bath every day, his skin would get dry and maybe even crack. That would let bad bacteria into the body. Instead, a bath every two or three days is enough.

Until your baby sister can sit up on her own, she'll need to be bathed very carefully. Baby bathtubs keep her sitting upright and safe. Even after that, youngsters should never be left alone in a bath.

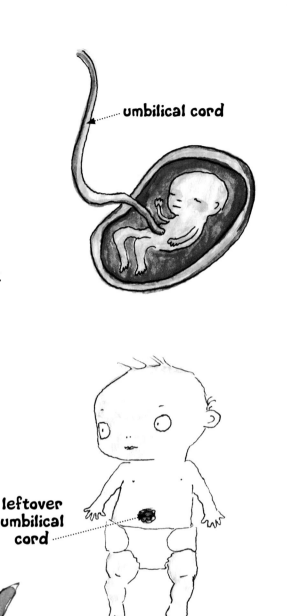
umbilical cord

During bath time, you might have noticed something brown and dry stuck to your baby brother's belly. That's called the **umbilical cord**. When he was inside Mom, the umbilical cord attached them together. The umbilical cord is how nutrients and blood traveled into his body. When he was born, the doctor or nurse (or maybe even Dad) cut the umbilical cord. It was no longer needed. But that brown bit of the cord was left stuck to brother's belly button. It falls off naturally after a few weeks.

leftover umbilical cord

If you have an outie belly button, it means a little more skin was left over when your umbilical cord healed. Humans aren't the only ones with belly buttons. Dogs, chimpanzees, and gorillas also have them!

rash

BUMPY BABY STUFF

Your baby brother's skin is very sensitive. He can even get pimples like your teenage cousin. Doctors suspect this is from changing hormones. It might be tempting to wash it with soap, but grownup face soaps will dry out his skin.

Babies can get a heat rash too. When a baby is too hot, it can develop tiny red blisters. This usually goes away on its own. To help avoid it, make sure your little bro is dressed in loose cotton clothing when it's hot!

pimples

Cradle cap is another weird thing babies get. It looks scaly and yellow or white. It mostly happens on the baby's head, though it can also appear on their neck, ears, or armpits. It doesn't bother the baby. If it bothers you, lightly brush the scalp with a soft baby brush. Then wash the baby's hair with a gentle shampoo. Baby oil can also help.

cradle cap

Some babies are born with a full head of hair that falls out after birth. When it grows back, it may be a different color.

TIME FOR TEETH

Babies are born with no teeth. Those gummy smiles are so cute, but they won't last long!

Twenty teeth begin developing while babies are still inside their mothers. They are below the gums and won't break through for a while. Your little sister will likely get her first tooth around six months of age. You might notice she drools more as her teeth grow. That's normal! Teeth are stronger than bones and can be painful as they break through the gums.

By the time your little bundle is three, she should have a mouth full of pearly whites. That won't last long! Baby teeth begin falling out around five years of age. They are replaced with adult teeth, which have to last for the rest of their life. That's why it's so important to take care of your teeth from the start!

If you notice your baby bro is getting fussy or having a hard time sleeping, it could mean a tooth is on the way. It sometimes helps to gently rub a clean finger along his gums. Teething rings can help too, especially if they are cool—but not frozen!

43

DON'T EAT THAT!

Why do babies put everything in their mouths?

As a newborn, the baby probably grabbed your finger or hair, but didn't do anything with it. It takes time to develop the ability to both hold and use an object. This skill begins to develop around three months. By seven months, large objects like blocks are easier to manage. But small things, like peas, take more time to handle.

Babies love putting things in their mouths. It's called "mouthing," and is something all babies do. They'll put anything in their mouths—even this book! That's why it's important to keep small things they could choke on out of their reach.

Mouthing helps babies learn to move their lips and tongues, which is handy for talking later on. It also helps prepare them for the task of chewing food and swallowing.

It's important to make sure baby toys are larger than 2¼ inches (5.5 centimeters) wide. Anything smaller must be out of a baby's reach. Foods like nuts, grapes, and candy are also dangerous.

DON'T PUT THAT IN YOUR NOSE!

Know what we all have in common? We've all picked boogers! It's a natural toddler behavior, and for some people—including adults—it's a disgusting habit.

Boogers are made of dried-up mucus, that slippery snot lining the inside of your nose. Dust, germs, dirt, and pollen all get trapped in the hairs in your nostrils. When the mucus dries up with all this stuff, it forms a crusty booger just begging to be picked.

Picking boogers once in a while is pretty harmless, unless you have dirty fingers. Bacteria might mix with the mucus and give you a cold.

Babies get boogers too. But they lack the fine motor skills to pick them. Instead of taking things out of their noses, babies sometimes shove things *into* their noses.

Doctors have found many objects stuck in babies' and toddlers' noses, like cherries, nuts, ladybugs, and pebbles. If the object isn't shoved too far in, then it isn't too much of a problem. But if it's wayyyyy up there, it's a good idea to have a doctor get it out.

Your nose will keep growing until about the time you turn eighteen. After that, it will start to droop as you grow older.

MAY I PLEASE BE EXCUSED?

It will be a while before your baby brother uses these kind of manners. Like everything else, communication must be practiced.

A baby's brain is ready to learn language. Babies are born with billions of **neurons**. Some will eventually control hearing and speech. Each time your baby brother hears words, those neurons become stronger. Even though babies are born with the ability to hear the differences between hundreds of sounds, they strengthen the connections for the language they hear most often.

Want to play with action figures?

Researchers believe it's important to make facial expressions for babies to imitate. Making a crazy, happy, or sad face helps babies imitate them and understand how to communicate emotions.

You've probably heard parents or other adults using "baby talk" with a new baby. It might be embarrassing, but it really helps the baby learn to speak. When you exaggerate sounds or speak slowly, it helps the baby understand the patterns of words. By the time the baby is twelve months old, he can tell which sounds are related to language. As the older, wiser person, you can do many things to help babies learn to talk.

NEW SOUNDS

The first sounds babies hear are **vowel** sounds like "oooo" and "ahhhh." Vowels are easier to say because we don't have to use our lips. The more you talk to your baby sister, the more she'll learn to copy different sounds.

Around five months of age, she'll start babbling. She's learning how to say **consonants**. Sometimes she'll just keep blurting "mamamamamamama" and you'll wonder if she'll ever stop. She's practicing. By the time she reaches seven months, she might recognize her name.

AAAHH

Mouse!

Mao!

Mouse?

Maowt!

That's right!

Around twelve months of age, many babies can say single words. They might point at something and want to know what it is. Soon, the words just start coming. By the end of their second year, toddlers can put words together and ask simple questions.

Hello Duckie!

I WANT A MUFFIN.

Some babies take longer to learn how to talk. This can get pretty frustrating. To help, learn **sign language**. Many babies have an easier time signing words than speaking them.

WOBBLY BABY!

It takes a long time for a baby's muscles to become strong enough for walking. Before they learn how to walk, most babies learn to **creep**, roll, sit up, and crawl on their own. Once they have the hang of that, standing and then walking will soon follow! And once your baby brother starts walking, it's only a matter of time before he's into *all* your stuff!

No!

One common danger for a small child is balloons. They might be great for parties, but they are dangerous choking hazards. Feel free to celebrate, but watch small children around them!

Babies fall a lot. Though you'll probably want to help her up, it's sometimes a good idea to let her get up on her own. It helps strengthen her muscles and learn on her own!

There are many new dangers in the home now that the baby is on the move. Look for things that can be climbed or pulled. Get on all fours and take a look around from a baby's height. What might interest them? Then make sure it's safe or out of reach!

Your sense of balance is connected to your eyes and ears. When you walk or move, your **vestibular (ves-TIB-you-lar) system** inside your ear works with other parts of your body to control movement. If you have an ear infection, you might feel dizzy and struggle to keep your balance.

HOW TO DEAL WITH TODDLERS

Once that sweet-smelling baby can walk and talk, she realizes she can do things on her own. The baby has officially become a **toddler**.

By the time a baby turns two, she'll have learned hundreds of new skills. But toddlers still need help doing many things. And that can be frustrating for them. You'll start to experience **tantrums**! That sweet lovey bear won't want to get in their car seat. Or put pants on. Or they want food RIGHT NOW!!!! Take a deep breath. It's all normal.

Waiting for something is hard for grownups too. Waiting for mom to come home, or for dessert after dinner, are hard things to understand.

Another hard concept for toddlers? The idea of "no." If they want that cookie, they want that cookie. Other times, the idea of "no" can be fun for toddlers, but miserable for the parents. It's almost impossible to put a floppy baby in a car seat. It's equally impossible to put clothes on a baby who refuses to get dressed!

Our brains don't stop developing when we become toddlers. In fact, a human brain isn't fully developed until about age twenty-five. Until then, humans don't always make the best choices.

TODDLER CHILLIN'

Sometimes your toddler sibling will do stuff that doesn't make much sense to you. It's hard to know just what that little person is up to, especially when they're around two or three years old.

One common toddler behavior that can seem odd at first is **self-soothing**. Toddlers (and sometimes teens and adults too!) often self-soothe when they are stressed out or even just chillin' out. The most famous form of toddler self-soothing is thumb-sucking. Some kids even slurp at *all* their fingers, like they're tasty chicken wings!

56

Another common toddler behavior is clinging to a favorite toy or stuffed animal that they CANNOT BE WITHOUT SO DON'T LOSE IT AND DON'T FORGET IT OR THE WHOLE WORLD WILL KNOW THAT JOHNNY CAN'T FIND MR. BUN-BUN!

In a pretty scary world, it helps to know you've got that comfy blanket Aunt Jen made or that favorite toy car from Uncle Jeff. It might not make sense to us, but it's important to them. Often it helps them feel safe, which is important. Over time, Mr. Bun-Bun will be forgotten . . . although that can be a sad day for parents!

It's not just toddlers who cling to objects. Some research suggests almost half of all adults still have their childhood snuggie. Some even admit to still sleeping with the object!

BEING A GOOD ROLE MODEL

Being the older child can be a drag sometimes. You have to be on your best behavior always so the baby doesn't become an evil genius. You become a gofer, getting the diaper cream or a burp rag for Mom or Dad. It might seem unfair.

But being the older child can also be awesome. Someone will always look up to you and think you are the best, smartest, most amazing person on the planet. You know how to buckle your own seat belt and tie your shoes! You're a genius in the eyes of your younger sibling!

With a new baby sister or brother in the house, you have the chance to correct any bad habits you have started to develop. Now washing your hands isn't just something your mom nags about. You know it's about keeping the baby healthy. And going to bed at a decent time isn't punishment. It helps you learn and grow.

So, while it's tough being the older kid, enjoy it while you can. That little one is going to grow up as fast as you did, and soon they'll want to do their own thing. When that happens, you'll miss how great it felt to be helpful.

GLOSSARY

bacteria—tiny single-cell bodies that live on every part of the earth and inside most people and animals. Some bacteria are harmful, while others are helpful for things like digestion.

behaviors—the usual actions of a person or animal

bile—a bitter liquid made inside an organ called the liver. Bile helps the body digest fats.

cartilage—a tough, white substance that is softer than bone but makes up part of the skeleton. Cartilage is also found in the nose and ears.

consonants—the letters that are not vowels (see opposite). Consonants usually have "hard" sounds.

creep—to move along on one's belly

degrade—to break down over time, such as a rotting apple or rusting can

deliver—to help a baby leave the mother's body at birth

diaphragm—a muscle inside the body just below the lungs

digestive system—a group of organs that helps a person or animal turn eaten food into energy

egg—a cell inside the mother that can develop into a baby when it combines with a male sperm cell

fontanelles—the soft areas between a baby's skull bones

formula—a special liquid fed to babies before they begin to eat solid foods

immune system—a group of organs that helps the body fight disease

meconium—a baby's first poop. Meconium is dark and sticky.

mucus—a slimy material that coats parts of the body, such as the inside of the nose or the throat

neurons—the special cells that form nerves and the brain. Electrical signals passing between neurons carry information to the brain.

nutrients—things in food that help people, animals, and plants grow and survive

organs—parts of a person, animal, or plant that do specific jobs. The brain, heart, and stomach are examples of animal organs.

rectum—opening at the end of the digestive system through which poop leaves the body

REM sleep—a stage of sleep during which most dreaming occurs

self-soothing—acts that people use to help calm themselves when stressed out

senses—the five ways in which animals experience their surroundings: 1) sight, 2) smell, 3) hearing, 4) taste, and 5) touch

sign language—a system of communication that uses hand signals rather than words or sounds

tantrums—outbursts of anger, usually from young children

toddlers—children who have just learned to walk, usually ages one to three

umbilical cord—a cord that connects a baby inside the womb to their mother. The womb carries nutrients from the mother to the baby.

vestibular system—bones, nerves, and tubes inside the ears that help people and animals balance

vowels—the letters A, E, I, O, and U

womb—the area inside a mother where a baby grows before it is born

INDEX

ABOUT THE AUTHOR AND ILLUSTRATOR

Julia Garstecki is a former elementary school teacher. She'd often find dried-up boogers stuck to desks. Now she teaches at Goodwin College, where her students have a tendency to binge on junk food and stay up too late. When Julia isn't teaching, she's researching new ideas for nonfiction books. And when she isn't doing that, she's nagging her kids about brushing teeth and turning off their screens. Julia's worst bad habit? Sharing her pillow with Bella, her toy poodle. She knows she shouldn't . . . but she can't help it!

Chris Monroe is the author of ten children's picture books, including *Pick, Spit & Scratch* and *Sniff, Lick & Scratch*. She is also the illustrator of picture books by authors Kevin Kling, Jane Yolen, and Janice Levy. Her comic strip, "Violet Days," was retired in 2018 after being in print for twenty-two years. Chris lives in Duluth, Minnesota.